PICTURE LIBRARY

MARTIAL
-ARTS-

PICTURE LIBRARY
MARTIAL
—ARTS—

Norman Barrett

Franklin Watts

London   New York   Sydney   Toronto

© 1988 Franklin Watts Ltd

First published in Great Britain
   1988 by
Franklin Watts Ltd
12a Golden Square
London W1R 4BA

First published in the USA by
Franklin Watts Inc
387 Park Avenue South
New York
NY 10016

First published in Australia by
Franklin Watts
14 Mars Road
Lane Cove
NSW 2066

UK ISBN: 0 86313 683 4
US ISBN: 0-531-10629-2
Library of Congress Catalog Card
Number 88-50361

Printed in Italy

Warning
The martial arts require a
disciplined and intelligent
approach. Many of the moves
and exercises may be dangerous.
Neither children nor adults
should attempt to copy any of
the techniques illustrated in
this book except under the
strict supervision of a
qualified instructor.

Designed by
Barrett & Willard

Photographs by
Peter Lewis
Action Plus
Japan National Tourist Organization
Chris McCooey
N.S. Barrett Collection
E.W.J. Stratton

Illustrations by
Rhoda & Robert Burns

Technical Consultant
Peter Lewis

Contents

Introduction

The martial arts are the fighting skills that have developed in the East over many hundreds of years. Some are practiced as a way of life, along with the religions of the East. Others emphasize self-defense or sports.

The secrets of the martial arts were largely unknown in the West until 30 or 40 years ago. Now, their popularity is widespread.

△ Judo, an Olympic event, is popular with all ages and both sexes. It is the sporting offshoot of ju-jitsu, an ancient form of warrior training. Judo authorities prefer judo to be thought of as a combat sport, rather than a martial art.

Many of the martial arts are practiced and studied to produce a healthy mind as well as a healthy body. Experts in the deadlier of the martial arts are sworn to use their skills only in self-defense.

   The spread of the martial arts to the West has been chiefly as sport.

△ The main features of karate are strikes and kicks to the body. In competition karate, actual contact is not permitted.

Looking at martial arts

Judo – stomach throw (tomoe-nage)

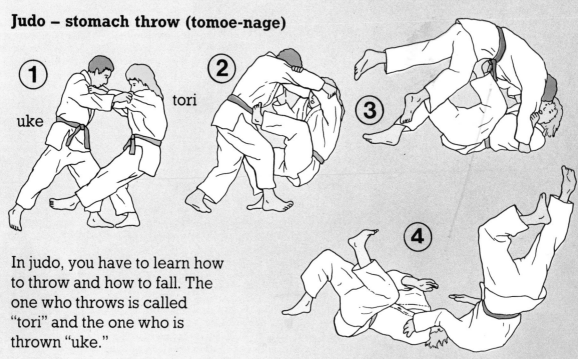

uke   tori

In judo, you have to learn how to throw and how to fall. The one who throws is called "tori" and the one who is thrown "uke."

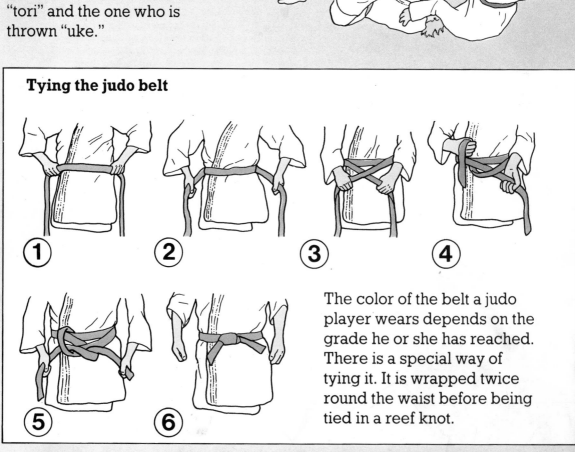

Tying the judo belt

The color of the belt a judo player wears depends on the grade he or she has reached. There is a special way of tying it. It is wrapped twice round the waist before being tied in a reef knot.

Karate – side kick

① ② ③

In karate sparring contests, blows are delivered with strength, but must be "pulled," stopped just short of the target. The legs are powerful weapons, and are used to strike at an opponent.

Kung fu stances

Leopard

Tiger

Dragon

Crane

Snake

The ancient Chinese used the fighting methods of animals, real or imaginary, as the basis of a system of martial arts. Many kung fu systems were based on the skills of five animals.

Karate

Karate is a Japanese form of unarmed combat. The word means "empty hands." But, as well as hands, the "karateka," or one who trains in karate, also uses legs, feet, elbows and even the head.

Sport karate comes from Shotokan, the most popular of the many styles of karate. There are two kinds of contests, "kata" and "kumite."

△ A front kick is blocked. In karate contests, blows are "pulled," or held back at the last moment. A karate contestant wears "karategi," light, loose-fitting jacket and trousers, with a colored belt showing his or her grade. The highest grade is entitled to wear a black belt.

Kata are a series of movements or routines performed by students. They consist of strikes, punches, kicks, blocks and stances. They are marked by judges who award points for technique and timing.

Kumite are sparring contests. They are carefully controlled, with the more dangerous blows prohibited. Judges award ippons (full points) or wazaris (half points) for well-executed attacking moves.

▽ Young students (left) learning karate techniques in a training class. A stylist in goju-ryu karate (right) demonstrates a knife hand block. Goju-ryu means "hard-soft," and is one of the many styles of karate.

◁ Experts demonstrate a side kick to the throat. Attacks to the throat, eyes, and joints are among those not permitted in sport karate.

▷ Weapons called kama are used as a training device in karate. They were developed from a farming tool called a sickle.

▽ A power-breaking demonstration. Tests called "tamashiwara" measure the power released by karate experts with blows from head, elbow or hand.

Kung fu

The martial arts of China are known as kung fu. A kung fu practitioner is one who works or exercises to the best of his or her ability.

There are many styles of kung fu, adapted to the type of person using it. As well as self-defense, they improve health and teach how to live in harmony with others.

Some kung fu styles include ideas from other systems, such as holds and throws. But most kung fu comes from the original five animal styles.

▽ A master of kung fu (left) teaches the finer points of attack and defense to a student. This style of kung fu is called wing chun, after its inventor, a nun called Yim Wing Chun. The movements of wing chun are based on those of the crane and the snake and are well suited for close-range fighting.

△ A group practicing
tai-chi. This is the
"softer" side of kung fu,
the fighting forms being
called the "hard" style.
Tai-chi means "grand
ultimate fist." All
movements are linked
together in a flowing
sequence. Tai-chi is a
healthy form of exercise
for both mind and body.

◁ The choy li fut style
of kung fu is a kind of
long-range kick boxing.
Power is generated
from the waist, and
kicks and punches are
delivered with great
force.

▷ Students in a kung fu class learning moves.

◁ Weapons are used in many kung fu styles for performing patterns, or routines, like the kata in karate. These include the three-section staff and a spear called a kwan-do (top left) and the butterfly knives (top right).

Even a master can learn a lesson (bottom left). Yip Chun, grandmaster of wing chun, teaches Samuel Kwok a thing or two.

Sport kung fu in action (bottom right). Semi- or full-contact kung fu is practiced in competition, with judges awarding points.

▷ The lion dance is a tradition seen in China and in other parts of the world with Chinese communities. It is performed only by people who practice kung fu.

Tae kwon do

Tae kwon do is a Korean style of unarmed combat, similar to karate, with great emphasis on strikes with hands and feet. "Tae" means to kick, "kwon" to punch and "do" means way or path. Tae kwon do is the most popular martial art in the United States. US servicemen, stationed in Korea during the 1950s, brought tae kwon do back with them when they returned to the United States.

△ Spectacular kicks are the hallmark of tae kwon do.

▷ Tae kwon do is practiced as a competitive sport and is judged like karate. It was accepted as a demonstration sport for the 1988 Olympic Games at Seoul, South Korea, where the headquarters of tae kwon do are situated.

Thai boxing

Thai boxing is the national sport of Thailand, but has spread to many other countries around the world.

Contestants may use their feet, knees and elbows as well as gloved fists. Contests take place in a boxing ring, and bouts last for five 3-minute rounds. They are won by a knock-out or by a decision.

In Thailand, young boys are introduced to the art of kick boxing before they can read or write.

▷ Thai boxing is probably the roughest of the martial arts. Years of hard training make the Thai boxer a complete fighting machine, rarely challenged by followers of other martial arts.

▽ Young pupils give a public demonstration of kick boxing. In the West, the more dangerous aspects of Thai boxing, such as elbow strikes, have been banned.

Ju-jitsu and judo

Ju-jitsu is an ancient Japanese martial art, used for both armed and unarmed combat. The basic principle of ju-jitsu is to turn an opponent's own strength and weight against him or her.

The locks and grips used in ju-jitsu can seriously injure or even kill a person. Students of ju-jitsu learn how to strangle, dislocate joints, break limbs and throw an opponent three times their own weight.

▽ Ju-jitsu is practiced only under the strictest supervision. The grips and locks are not applied to the full extent. The threat of injury is enough to persuade an opponent to submit.

Judo is a sport that was developed from ju-jitsu. It means "the gentle way." The object is to throw your opponent cleanly on his or her back, or force a submission. Bouts may also be decided on a points system.

A judo player is called a "judoka." Judo is played barefoot in a loose-fitting jacket and trousers called a "judogi." In championship judo, the players compete at separate weights.

△ The chief skill in judo is to catch your opponent off balance and use his or her weight to your advantage.

Aikido

Aikido means "the way of all harmony." Like judo, it developed from ju-jitsu. But aikido uses only defensive techniques. The chief object of aikido is to bring together mind, body and a hidden source of energy known as "ki."

There are several styles of aikido and types of competition. The contestants usually take turns to be the "tori," or defender. In some contests, the "uke," or attacker, is armed with a rubber knife.

▽ The defender in aikido uses his opponent's own movements to throw him to the ground. He makes particular use of the attacker's wrist and elbow joints.

Other martial arts

△ Two women with swords demonstrate a style of wu shu, a Chinese martial art.

◁ Sumo wrestling is an ancient Japanese sport steeped in the rituals of the Shinto religion. The huge wrestlers, built up on special diets, try to throw their opponents to the floor or push them out of the ring.

△ Ninja practice the art of ninjitsu. They rely on natural body movements.

▷ A ninja hides in the bushes, ready to attack. The ninja were trained as spies and assassins in ancient Japan. From boyhood they learned the arts of stealth, camouflage, survival and armed and unarmed combat. The word ninja means "stealers-in."

◁ Escrima, or stick-fighting. A style of kali, the Filipino martial arts, it is particularly popular in the United States.

▽ Kendo is the Japanese sport of sword-fighting. The swords, called "shinai," are made of bamboo. Before a bout begins, the contestants observe the traditional ceremonies of the samurai, the Japanese warriors of feudal times.

The story of martial arts

Fights to the death

Fighting as a sport goes back to the days of the ancient Greeks, over 2,000 years ago. The ancient Olympics included an event called the pankration. This was a

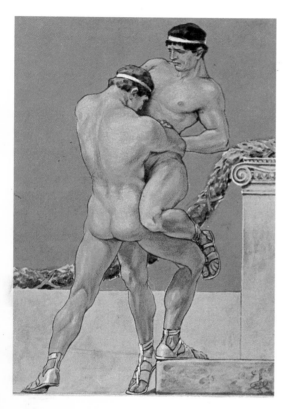

△ The ancient Greeks developed wrestling as a sport in their Olympic Games over 2,000 years ago.

no-holds-barred contest in which the combatants could strike their opponents with feet, fists, elbows and knees. The winner of a bout was the one left standing, while the loser was often seriously maimed or even left to die.

Unarmed combat

Various fighting styles came out of the cruel pankration. The Greeks developed boxing and wrestling skills, and these sports flourished in the West.

It is known that conquering armies of the Greek leader Alexander the Great spread skills of pankration eastward. From these and the fighting methods that must have existed in the East, many different styles of unarmed combat developed.

Religion and secrecy

For hundreds of years the Eastern martial arts developed under religious influences. They became a way of life, a part of the eastern religions of Buddhism, Confucianism and Taoism. Sumo wrestling, which is possibly 2,000 years old, stems from the

△ Sumo wrestling in Japan in the 1860s, as seen by a Western artist.

△ A pose from the system of kung fu called Shaolin fist, which originated in the Shaolin Temple in China hundreds of years ago.

Japanese Shinto religion. Most of the secrets of the martial arts remained hidden to Western eyes until the 20th century.

Kung fu and karate

Kung fu goes back some 2,000 years. It is said to have originated in the Shaolin Temple, in northern China. Originally there were five styles, based on the movements of animals. Now there are thousands of different styles.

Karate is a mixture of kung fu and the fighting arts of the island of Okinawa. The islanders developed karate in the last century to resist the invading Japanese. Modern karate was developed by Gichin Funakoshi in the 1920s.

Development of judo

Ju-jitsu originated in Japan, perhaps as the deadliest of the martial arts. But out of it came judo and aikido, which preach self-defense rather than attack. In 1964 judo was accepted as a sport in the modern Olympic Games.

△ A Japanese expert (right) demonstrates the art of ju-jitsu with a Western wrestler. Out of ju-jitsu came judo, now an Olympic sport.

Spread to the West

The great popularity of the martial arts in the West is due largely to Bruce Lee and the films he made in the 1970s. These brought the secrets of kung fu to the West, and since then other martial arts, such as ninjitsu, have also spread across the world.

Facts and records

The belt system

Students of karate and judo are graded according to their ability. Their grade is denoted by a colored belt. Students take an examination every few months, and if successful are promoted to the next kyu (student) grade. The belt colors are as follows, although in some styles of karate they may vary:

	karate	judo
novice	red	white
9th kyu	—	yellow
8th kyu	white	orange
7th kyu	yellow	orange
6th kyu	orange	green
5th kyu	green	green
4th kyu	purple	blue
3rd kyu	brown	blue
2nd kyu	brown	brown
1st kyu	brown	brown

Dan (advanced) grades are denoted by black belts, progressing from 1st dan to 10th dan.

The big men

Sumo wrestlers are the heaviest of all sportsmen, many of them weighing more than 160 kg (350 pounds). Few foreigners succeed in this Japanese sport. But by the late 1980s an American, Salevaa Fuauli Atisonoe from Hawaii, had

△ Konishiki, from Hawaii, the heaviest sumo wrestler ever.

fought his way to the rank of ozeki (great barrier), just below the top rank of yokozuna (grand champion). At over 240 kg (520 pounds), and fighting under the ring name of Konishiki, he became the heaviest sumo wrestler ever.

Weight divisions

The Japanese always believed that weight did not matter in judo, only skill. But in 1961 a 120 kg (264 pounds) Dutchman, Anton Geesink, defeated all three Japanese players to win the world title. Since then, weight divisions have been introduced into championship judo.

Glossary

Aikido
A Japanese martial art that uses only defensive techniques.

Dan
An advanced grade in some martial arts.

Escrima
A Filipino art of fighting with double sticks. It is an old Spanish word for "skirmish."

Judo
A branch of ju-jitsu that has developed as a combat sport. It means "the gentle way."

Ju-jitsu
A Japanese martial art in which an opponent's strength is used against him or her.

Kali
Filipino martial arts.

Karate
A Japanese martial art using strikes and kicks. It means "empty hands."

Kendo
Japanese sword-fighting.

Kung fu
The words mean "good effort"

and although the term was originally applied to the Chinese martial arts by Westerners, it is now used by the Chinese themselves.

Kyu
A student grade in some martial arts.

Ninja
A person trained in ninjitsu.

Ninjitsu
A stealthy Japanese martial art that uses natural body movements.

Sumo wrestling
The traditional Japanese style of wrestling.

Tae kwon do
A Korean style of unarmed combat.

Tai-chi
A style of kung fu practiced chiefly as an exercise for mind and body.

Wing chun
A style of kung fu based on the movements of the crane and the snake. The words mean "beautiful springtime."

Index